Songs for Choirs

This collection of songs has been designed to provide a wide range of suitable material for mixed choirs of varying ability. Whilst the pianoforte accompaniment is an essential part of some of the pieces, in the others it is optional, and may well be disregarded by choirs to whom unaccompanied singing presents no difficulties.

CONTENTS

© Oxford University Press 1972

Oxford University Press
Music Department, Walton Street, Oxford OX2 6DP

2

1. NATURE CAROL
(Filipino Plantation Song)

Words and music
arranged by
MALCOLM SARGENT

From *Three Far-Eastern Carols* (O.U.P. X73).

Songs for Choirs

Hawaii 1960

3. *mf* Meadow, orchard, field and vine,
   Melon, grape and maize are here,
   Leaf and sheaf with tendrils twine,
   Bring your harvests from far and near.
   ff Alohā! Hanaw, etc.

4. *f* Mountains, flowers, trees and hills,
   Laugh and sing where His blessings fall,
   Wind and waves, lagoons and rills,
   Shout his love who is Lord of all.
   ff Alohā! Hanaw, etc.

★ Alohā, pronounced 'Al-oh-hah' = 'greetings'
Hanaw, pronounced 'Hah-now' = 'Dear little one'
The tenors and basses do not sing the first word in each verse.

Songs for Choirs

4

2. KALINKA

Words by
A.M.P. and T.B.P.

Russian folk-song
arranged by J. KIRK

Kalinka pronounced *Kaleenka*
The piano introduction and ending are optional.

Songs for Choirs

To the choir of Portway School, Bristol

3. KWMBAYAH

African tune
arranged by K. J. DINHAM

★The word 'kwmbayah' should always be sung *pesante*, even when *ppp*.

The tune is from *Weaver's Song Book* by permission.

This arrangement is published separately, but with Christmas words (O.U.P. X186).

- ah! Some - one's pray - ing, Lord, kym - bay - ah! Some - one's

pray - ing, Lord, kym - bay - ah!___ O___ Lord, kym - bay - ah!

In strict time

3. Al - le - lu - ia, Lord! kym - bay - ah! Al - le - lu - ia, Lord, kym - bay -

- ah! Al - le - lu - ia, Lord, kym - bay - ah! O___ Lord, kym - bay - ah!

4. I GOT A ROBE

Negro spiritual
arranged by J. KIRK

The piano introduction and ending are optional.

10

5. HO-LA-HI

Trans. R.F.

German folk-song
arranged by ROGER FISKE

Songs for Choirs

16

(Two or three voices)

Songs for Choirs

18

6. MEN OF HARLECH

Welsh traditional song
arranged by
C. ARMSTRONG GIBBS

Hark, I hear the foe ad-van-cing, Bar-bèd steeds are proud-ly pran-cing,
Men of Har-lech, lie ye dream-ing? See ye not their fal-chions gleam-ing?

Hel-mets, in the sun-beams glan-cing, glit-ter through the trees.
While their pen-nants, gai-ly stream-ing, flut-ter in the

From *Suite of Songs from the British Isles* arr. C. Armstrong Gibbs (O.U.P.)
The complete work is scored for orchestra, and for strings and piano.
Material is on hire.

Songs for Choirs

20

ar - rows fly - ing scat-ter sud - den death. Fright - ened steeds are
mer - cy pray-ing

with their part-ing breath. See, they're in dis - or - der.

See, they're in___ dis-

Com - rades, keep close or - der. Ev - er they shall rue the day They
- or - der. Com - rades, keep close.

Songs for Choirs

22

Now the Sax - on

ven - tured o'er the bor - der. Now___ the Sax - - on flees be - fore us,

ff

Now the Sax - on

Vic - t'ry's ban - ner float - eth o'er us. Raise the loud ex -

rit.

- ul - ting chor - us, "Bri - tain wins the field."_____

rit.

7. THE LONE STAR TRAIL

American Cowboy song
arranged by PETER RELF

Songs for Choirs

26

Songs for Choirs

8. SLOOP JOHN B

Arranged by
PETER RELF

Songs for Choirs

34

Songs for Choirs

took him a - way. Oh! Mis - ter John-stone,
took him a - way. Oh! Mis - ter John-stone,
- way. Oh! Mis - ter John - stone, Please let me go
- way. Oh! Mis - ter John - stone, Please let me go

Please let me go home, I feel so broke up, I wan-na go home.
Please let me go home, I'm broke up, I wan-na go home.
home, I'm broke up, I wan-na go home.
home, I'm broke up, I wan-na go home.

Songs for Choirs

9. IF YOU'LL MARRY ME

(from *The Sorcerer*)

W. S. GILBERT

ARTHUR SULLIVAN

Published by arrangement with J. B. Cramer & Co. Ltd.

Songs for Choirs

43

take you in and do for you. All this will I do if you'll mar-ry me!

All this will I do if you'll mar-ry me! Eh!_____ Eh! but I

do like you!

Songs for Choirs

10. NOW TO THE BANQUET WE PRESS

(from *The Sorcerer*)

W. S. GILBERT

ARTHUR SULLIVAN

Now to the ban-quet we press, Now for the eggs and the ham!

Now for the mus-tard and cress, Now for the straw-ber-ry jam!

Published by arrangement with J. B. Cramer & Co. Ltd.

Songs for Choirs

Now for the tea of our host!___ Now for the rol-lick-ing bun!___

Now for the muf-fin and toast, And now for the gay Sal - ly Lunn!___

Now for the muf-fin and toast, And now for the gay Sal - ly Lunn! The

p

Songs for Choirs

46

Songs for Choirs

straw - ber - ry jam, And the rol - lick - ing bun! The

rol - lick-ing bun And the gay Sal - ly Lunn And the straw - ber - ry

jam, jam,

jam, bun, bun, Oh! the straw - ber-ry, straw - ber-ry

48

Songs for Choirs

11. YOU SPOTTED SNAKES

SHAKESPEARE

R. J. S. STEVENS
(1757 – 1837)

50

Songs for Choirs

f
blind-worms, do no wrong, Come not near_ our_ fai - ry queen;_ Come not
f
blind-worms, do no wrong,_ Come not near our fai - ry queen;_ Come not
f
blind-worms, do no wrong, Come not near our fai - ry queen; Come not
f
blind-worms, do no wrong, Come not near our fai - ry queen; Come not
f
A
near_ our fai - ry queen:
p
near our fai - ry_ queen:_ Phi - lo - mel_ with me - lo - dy,_
p
near our fai - ry queen: Sing_ in_
p
near our fai - ry queen: Sing_
A
p

Songs for Choirs

52

Songs for Choirs

53

Songs for Choirs

54

Songs for Choirs

12. HARK! HARK! THE LARK

SHAKESPEARE

BENJAMIN COOKE
(1734—1793)

water at those springs, On cha - lic'd flow'rs that lies;

springs, On cha - - - lic'd flow'rs____ that lies;

at those springs, On cha - lic'd flow'rs that lies;

lies;____ And wink - ing Ma - ry buds ____ be -

lies;____ And wink - ing Ma - ry buds ____ be -

lies;____ And wink - ing Ma - ry buds____ be -

gold - - en eyes, And wink - ing

- gin ____ to ope, wink - ing Ma - ry buds be - gin to ope____ their

- gin to ope, _____ be - gin to ope____ their

- gin _____ to

gold - - en eyes; My____

gold - en eyes; that pret - ty is, My

gold - - en eyes;

13. HOW BLEST ARE SHEPHERDS
(King Arthur)

HENRY PURCELL

Moderato

SOPRANO
1. How blest are shep-herds, how hap-py their lass-es,
2. Bright nymphs of Brit-ain, with gra-ces at-tend-ed,

ALTO
1. How blest are shep-herds, how hap-py their lass-es,
2. Bright nymphs of Brit-ain, with gra-ces at-tend-ed,

TENOR
1. How blest are shep-herds, how hap-py their lass-es,
2. Bright nymphs of Brit-ain, with gra-ces at-tend-ed,

BASS
1. How blest are shep-herds, how hap-py their lass-es,
2. Bright nymphs of Brit-ain, with gra-ces at-tend-ed,

PIANO

While drums and trum-pets are sound-ing a-larms.
Let not your days with-out plea-sure ex-pire.

While drums and trum-pets are sound-ing a-larms.
Let not your days with-out plea-sure ex-pire.

While drums and trum-pets are sound-ing a-larms.
Let not your days with-out plea-sure ex-pire.

While drums and trum-pets are sound-ing a-larms.
Let not your days with-out plea-sure ex-pire.

★ In the original version, each half-verse is first sung by a tenor soloist singing the melody (soprano line), the full chorus singing the repeat.

Songs for Choirs

(1.) O - ver our low - ly sheds all the storm pass - es,
(2.) Hon - our's but emp - ty, and when youth is end - ed,

Foe - men may fight and die 'mid clash of arms,
All men may praise you, though none will ad - mire,

All the day on our herds and flocks em - ploy - ing,
Let not youth fly a - way with - out con - sent - ing,

All the night on our flutes mu - sic en - joy - ing.
Age will come time e - nough for your re - pent - ing.

* In the original version, each half-verse is first sung by a tenor soloist singing the melody (soprano line), the full chorus singing the repeat.

Songs for Choirs

14. IN OUR DEEP VAULTED CELL

(Dido and Aeneas)

HENRY PURCELL

The small notes in brackets should be sung as an echo and by a semichorus if possible.

Songs for Choirs

15. DESTRUCTION'S OUR DELIGHT

(Dido and Aeneas)

HENRY PURCELL

16. THEN ROUND ABOUT THE STARRY THRONE

(Samson)

G.F. HANDEL

74

Songs for Choirs

17. RING A DING A DING

J. KIRK

The piano introduction is optional.

Songs for Choirs

18. JESUS, MY JESUS

J. KIRK

The piano introduction is optional.

Songs for Choirs

Processed and printed by
Halstan & Co. Ltd., Amersham, Bucks., England